Sentence Generation

Syntax Tree Diagram in English, Spanish, Chinese, Japanese, Ainu

Yuko Sakai

SENTENCE GENERATION vol.1
CreateSpace Independent Publishing Platform
Copyright © 2017 Yuko Sakai
All rights reserved.
ISBN: 1545429006
ISBN-13: 978-1545429006

PREFACE

This work aims to present in outline a linguistic theory according to the sentence generation based on the view that the nature of language is to express cognition. While language is expression of cognition, how should be a sentence? Deducing the sentence structure of cognition, we verify the structure inductively in various phenomena in some languages.

In the first, we will look at the relation between cognition and sentence, especially in relation to universal sentence structure, which may correspond to so-called the DEEP STRUCTURE OF SENTENCE or "semantic absolutes, known in advance of grammar" (Chomsky 1957:101, NB 9) by Noam Chomsky. The grammars vary from language to language not only synchronically but diachronically. If we find something universal in language, we have to begin at the contents before the forms. The Aristotle's traditional grammar begins in the forms of the language and the contents are to be interpreted from the forms in reverse order to the logical process of sentence generation. We should begin not at the tips of branches, but the trunk of a tree following the scientific logic.

Secondly, we will see the SURFACE STRUCTURE OF SENTENCE in English, Spanish, Chinese, Japanese and Ainu; the language of the Japanese indigenous people in the crisis of the extinction, in the same framework of the UNIVERSAL SENTENCE STRUCTURE. Perceiving the same thing we express it in various languages according to their own rules or grammars. We will see their reason based on the universal sentence structure defining each word in the syntax tree diagram just like the chemical formula, which explains what the material is by clarifying the structure of the limited elements on the Earth.

After the examination, finally we conclude what is the language with some prospects for future research.

CONTENTS

I   Structure of Cognition and Sentence Structure

1 Process of Sentence Generation

We perceive a thing by some of the five senses and recognize it by naming, where a language generates. We have no name for which we have never perceived such as the color of ultraviolet or ultrared. Fictions or false; Pegasus, Chimera, mermaid, etc., are artificial combinations or deformation of real things. And, some of the sentences may be communicated with any luck after the generation. First of all, language is an expression of cognition and, it may be communicated secondly.

(1) Process of Sentence Generation

Thing → Perception → Cognition = Language → (Communication)
<Contents+Sound>

In present-day science it is generally assumed that in our perceptible world a thing exists in four-dimensional space-time. If time forms a line, it has two extremes; the beginning and end. As time is invisible, the two extremes are recognized as two things, without either of which we can neither qualify nor quantify time. As time goes by, things change. When it does not change, it is also a static state of change. In this meaning time is a synonym of 'change.' We recognize a change by making a comparison between two things, before and after the change. The two things at both ends of time or change are axial parties in the structure of the four dimensions. When there are parties concerned, there must be a third party, in distinction from which the parties concerned stand out. As a matter of course a change causes interests, both advantageous and disadvantageous, which always arise in the third party.

The four dimensions cannot be a simple addition of three and one, but a whole structure in which time relates the three things, the two parties concerned and the third party. Space and time, the beginning and end, the parties concerned and the third party, all these in antithesis presuppose the existence of each other. Neither of them is recognized without the other. To recognize a thing means to relate it with the other things in the four-dimensional structure. Therefore, all cognition should be composed of this complete four-dimensional structure. We understand even a one-word sentence, because we have known the latent words.

When language expresses cognition, we will be able to find a correspondence between the units of cognition and language. Consequently, the structure of cognition should correspond to that of sentences. The first thing recognized at the beginning of time is expressed in the subject. The change or time is expressed in the verb, using the traditional term. But when the verb is a part of speech the same as a noun, adjective, adverb, etc., the logical category requires another name, for example, VERJECT. The end of the change is expressed in the direct object and the third party in the indirect object.

(2) Structure of Four-dimensional Cognition and Sentence Structure

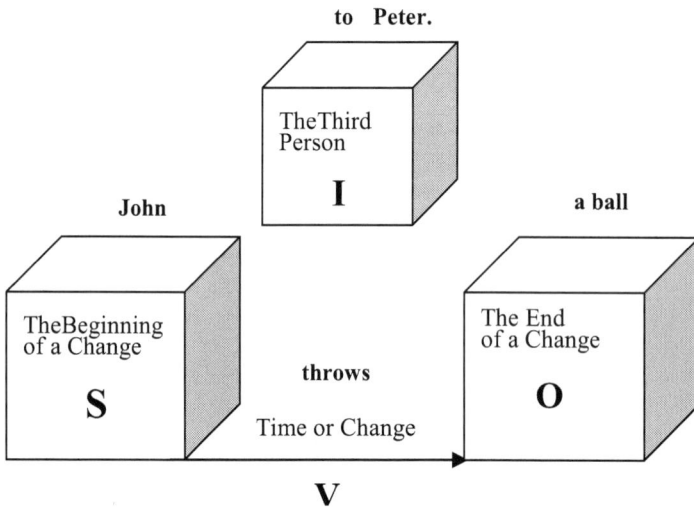

to   Peter.

The Third
Person

I

John

a ball

The Beginning
of a Change

S

throws

Time or Change

The End
of a Change

O

V

2 Deep Structure of Sentence

Based on the structure of cognition, the DEEP STRUCTURE OF SENTENCE or UNIVERSAL SENTENCE STRUCTURE can be represented as in (3).

This four-dimensional structure may be expressed as a line. But no special order is observed here, because the four-dimensional structure is captured as a whole in relativity and there are many ways to project it as a line.

(3) Universal Sentence Structure (order not specified)

$$\left[\begin{array}{c} S \\ V \\ I \\ O \end{array}\right.$$

3 Necessary Parts of Speech

A thing is expressed by a noun, which may be concrete or abstract. Accordingly, there must be nouns in any language to express the three correlative things.

The subjects and direct objects may be animate or inanimate, but, the indirect objects, which enjoy the interest of change for good or ill, should be animate. Though the indirect objects tend to have a similar form to adverb of place, the animacy distinguishes them.

While a thing cannot exist without time, there must be also the part to express the time, which is a verb.

If a thing is composed of quality and quantity and situated in space-time, all the attributes of a thing should belong to the quality, quantity or location in space and time. Therefore, the attributes are QUALIFIERS, QUANTIFIERS, SPATIALS or TEMPORALS. As a change is realized in a thing, the same can be seen in the attributes of a change or time, which are also to be ascribed to quality, quantity, and spatial and temporal location. Accordingly, all components of the four-dimensional structure, the three things and time, have extension of quality and quantity in spatial and temporal locations. The subject, direct object and indirect object are expressed as nouns, and the verject as a verb. Then, nouns and verbs are extended as modifiers based on four-dimensional relativity. In other words, all the modifiers of both nouns and verbs attribute to the four elements.

We can say that a noun is a bundle of some adjectives, and, a verb is a bundle of some adverbs. The modifiers are not added to the noun or verb, but extracted from them.

On account of the paucity of lexical meaning in the verb "be" it requires a complement (C) as an adverbial modifier to express a static existence, which may be a noun or adjective or adverb regardless of the parts of speech.

Consequently, the deep structure with modifiers should be as in (4-5).

(4) Adjectival Modifiers (order not specified)

```
        ┌(Qualifier Adjective) what (kind of)
        ├(Quantifier Adjective) how much/many
        ├(Temporal Adjective) of when
        ├(Spatial Adjective) of where
    Noun
```

(5) Adverbial Modifiers (order not specified)

```
    Verb
        ├  C  twhat/who /how/when/where/how much/many
        ├(Qualifier Adverb) how
        ├(Quantifier Adverb) how much
        ├(Temporal Adverb) when
        └(Spatial Adverb) where
```

3

(6) Parts to Express Universal Structure			
	Parts	Contents	
S	Nominals (+Adjectivals)	[+animate]	[-animate]
O			
I			
V	Verbals (+Adverbials)	Change of Quality	
		Change of Quantity	
		Change of Place	
		Change of Time	

II Surface Structure in English, Spanish, Chinese, Japanese, Ainu

The sentence structure shown in (3) and its extension shown in (4-5) are deduced from the necessity of cognition. These formulas should be present in any language, as far as language is an expression of cognition, and they should be induced from all languages. A theory is an attempt to explain reality, which proves and develops the theory.

However, in this short paper our intention is to sketch the theory, and as an example, we will try to explain some sentences in English, Spanish, Chinese, Japanese, Ainu.

1 Basic Sentence Structure

1) Components
The following is not more than a rough drawing, which allows more variations and needs more elaboration.

Ax; auxiliary verbs
Pro-; substitutes
+Q; interrogatives
-s; information about S such as conjugation
-x/x-; noun marks such as prepositions or postpositions (particles)
+3; 3rd person
-3; not 3rd person

The Chinese proper name is generally composed of monosyllabic first and second names.

About the change of word order caused by pronominalization we will see later.

(7) English
┌ S   John
├ V-s sends
├ I   Mary
└ O   flowers.

(8) Spanish
┌ S   Juan
├ V-s envía
├ O   flores
└ x-I a María.

(9) Chinese
- S 张伟 Zhāng Wěi
- V 送 sòng
- I 王芳 Wáng Fang
- O 花. huā

(10) Japanese
- S-x 弘が Hiroshi-ga
- I-x 洋子に Yoko-ni
- O-x 花を hana-o
- V 送る。okru (send)

(11) Ainu (mainly of Saru region)
- S Nanke'aynu
- I Sátamo
- O nonno
- V eikra. (send)

2) Modifiers

The word order may be a standard and it may change depending on the context. The meaning is somewhat unnatural to show the order of the adjectives. For example, in English "village men" is much less frequent than "villagers".

In Chinese, the modifier "ancient" is acceptable, it sounds unnatural.

We have not found any Ainu example with so many adjectivals and the chart shows merely a possibility.

a. Adjectives

(12) English
- (Aj-Qt) many
- (Aj-Ql) great
- (Aj-T) ancient
- (Aj-Ql) old
- (Aj-P) village
Noun men

(13) Spanish
- (Aj-Qt) muchos
- (Aj-Ql) grandes (great)
Noun hombres
- (Aj-Ql) viejos (old)
- (Aj-P) del pueblo
- (Aj-T) del antaño

(14) Chinese
- (Aj-Qt) 许多 xǔduō
- (Aj-Ql) 伟大的 wěidà de(great)
- (Aj-Ql) 老 lǎo (old)
- (Aj-Ql) (古 gǔ (ancient))
- (Aj-P) 村 cūn
Noun 民 mín

(15) Japanese
- (Aj-Qt) 多くの ooku-no
- (Aj-Ql) 偉大な idaina (great)
- (Aj-Ql) 老齢の rourei-no (old)
- (Aj-T) 昔の mukashi-no
- (Aj-P) 村- mura-
Noun 人 bito たち tachi [pl.]

(16) Ainu
  ┌(Aj-T) teeta
  ├(Aj-Qt) poro
  ├(Aj-Ql) pase (great)
  ├(Aj-Ol) onne (old)
  ├(Aj-P) kotan ta an (village at be)
Noun utar

b. Adverbs

(17) English
  V   swam
  ├(Av-Qt) a lot
  ├(Av-T) today
  ├(Av-Ql) happily
  └(Av-P) in the river.

(18) Spanish
  V   nadé (I swam)
  ├(Av-Qt) mucho
  ├(Av-T) hoy
  ├(Av-Ql) felizmente
  └(Av-P) en el río.

(19) Chinese
  ┌(Av-T) 今天 jīntiān
  ├(Av-P) 在河里 zài hé lǐ
  ├(Av-Ql) 快乐地 kuàilè de
  V 游泳 yóuyǒng
  └(Av-Qt)很久. hěnjiǔ
       (long time)

(20) Japanese
  ┌(Av-T) 今日 kyou
  ├(Av-P) 川で kawa-de
  ├(Av-Ql) 楽しく tanoshiku
  ├(Av-Qt) たくさん takusaN
  V 泳いだ。 oyoida

(21) Ainu
  ┌(Av-T) tanto
  ├(Av-P) pet or ta (river place in)
  ├(Av-Qt) poronno
  ├(Av-Ql) eramasuno
  V sus.

3) Parts of Speech

The following parts of speech are not based on the form, but on the contents to express the universal parts; noun, adjective, verb and adjective. Therefore, for example, a formal noun modifying another noun is not a noun but an adjective.

a. Nouns and Verbs

The nouns to express the deep structure are not only the formal nouns, but also other nominals, as we see in the following table.

(22) English Nnouns and Verbs			Examples
N	Nouns	[concrete nouns]	apple, book
		[abstract nouns]	liberty, importance
		Noun clauses	(the fact) (that) you won the race
		Infinitives [with *to*]	to run
		Infinitives [without *to*]	(Let me) go.
		Gerund	swimming
	Pronouns	Referential	I, you, he, she, it, this, that
		Interrogative-Exclamatory	What, who, which
		Relative	which , that
V	(Aux.+) Verbs		(do/will etc.) come
	Pro-verbs		(You knew him before I) did.

Using one stem for two words, the gender in Spanish economizes the vocabulary and relates the words semantically; "hermano/a (brother/sister)", "puerto/a (port/door)", "ventana/o (window/little window), "manzana/o (apple/apple tree)" etc.

(23) Spanish Nouns and Verbs			Examples
N	Nouns	[concrete nouns]	manzana, libro
		[abstract nouns]	libertad, importancia
		Noun clauses	(el hecho de) (que) ganaste la carrera
		Infinitives	correr, ir, nadar
	Pronouns	Referential	yo, tú, él, ella, éste, ése, aquel
		Interrogative-Exclamatory	qué, quién, cuál
		Relative	que, cual
V	Verbs		vengo, vienes...

All the Chinese words are monosyllabic morphemes, which may be various parts of speech. For example, 书 shū may be "write (verb)", "writing (adverb/noun)", "written (adjective)", "to write (noun)", "document (noun)", "book (noun)" etc., depending on its word order, similar to English noun and verb "book". The four tones, or more tones in dialects, serve to distinguish the meaning of monosyllabic words.

(24) Chinese Nouns and Verbs			Examples
N	Nouns	[concrete nouns]	苹果 píngguǒ (apple), 书 shū (book)
		[abstract nouns]	自由 zìyóu (libety), 重要性 zhòngyào xìng (importance)
		Noun clauses	(事实上) 你赢得了比赛 (shìshí shàng (as fact)) nǐ yíngdéle bǐsài (you won the race)
	Pronouns	Referential	我 wǒ (I), 你 nǐ (you), 他 tā (he), 她 tā (she), 它 tā (it), 这个 zhège (this), 那个 nàgè (that)
		Interrogative-Exclamatory	什么 shénme (what), 谁 shuí (who), 哪一个 nǎ yīgè (which)
V	(Aux. +) Verbs		会 huì(will) 来 lái (come)

In Japanese, most of nouns and verbs are written in Kanji (Chinese character), and grammatical markers are written in Hiragana; letters originated in Japan from Kanji by women. The Kanji of basic nouns and verbs has the proper Japanese pronunciation, and, the pronunciation of the conceptual nouns and verbs are adopted from ancient Chinese pronunciation. Occidental nouns or verbs, and their omitted forms, are written in Katakana with the bisyllabic sound patter of CVCV basically; personal computer>パソコン pasokoN, smart phone>スマホ sumaho.

(25) Japanese Nouns and Verbs			Examples
N	Nouns	[concrete nouns]	りんご riNgo(apple), 本 hoN (book)
		[abstract nouns]	自由 jiyuu (liberty), 重要性 juuyousei (importance)
		Noun clauses	あなたが競争に勝ったこと anata-ga (you) kyouso-ni (at race) katta (won) koto (thing), 走ること hashiru (run) koto(thing), 行くこと iku(go) (thing)
	Pronouns	Referential	私 watashi (I), あなた anata (you), 彼 kare (he), 彼女 kanojo (she), これ kore (this), それ sore (that), あれ are (that)
		Interrogative-Exclamatory	何 nani (what), 誰 dare (who), どれ dore (which)
V	(Aux.＋) Verbs		来る kuru (come) (だろう darou (will etc.))

The vocabulary of Ainu language does not correspond to that of other modern language. Similar to Chinese, most of Ainu words are monosyllabic and, a word tends to be composed of some words, for example, "káni" (I) is derived from an adverb phrase ku=an-i (I=be-so), "cep" (fish), from an adjective phrase c (i)=e-p (we=eat-thing), "aep"(food), from an adjective phrase a=e-p (one=eat-thing) etc. The collocated composition of monosyllabic words serves to distinguish the homonymy in Ainu instead of tones in Chinese.

(26) Ainu Nouns and Verbs			Examples
N	Nouns	[concrete nouns]	setani (little wild apple), kanpisos (book)
		[abstract nouns]	nu (good fishing), siri(appearance)
		Noun clauses	e=kattaro (you win)
		Infinitives	hoyupu(to run), arpa(to go), ma(to swim)
	Pronouns	Referential	káni, eani, sinuma (he, she; seldom used), tap(this), toanpe (that)
		Interrogative-Exclamatory	hemanta (what), hunna (who), inan-pe (which-one)
V	Verbs		ek (come) (nankor (will [particle]))

b. Adjectives

As the definite articles substitute all the modifiers of nouns, they are pro-adjectives; <u>a pretty little red riding</u> hood > <u>the</u> hood. The indefinite articles show the absence of the information to be substituted. Therefore, they are also pro-adjectives which substitute zeroes information.

(27) English Adjectives		Examples
Qualifier		white, long, big
Adjectives	Prepositive Nouns	post (office)
	Possessive Adjectives	children's (song)
	Adjective Phrases	(a picture) of great value
	Adjective Clauses	(the door) (that) you opened
	Infinitives	(the room) to be cleaned
	Present Particles	laughing (children)
	Past Particles	ironed (shirt)
Quantifier		much/many, few, no (money)
Adjectives	Cardinal Number djectives	one, two, three
	Multiple Adjectives	double, triple
Adjectives		urban, arctic
of Place	Ordinal Number Adjectives	first, second, third
	Prepositive Nouns	north (wind) (; wind from the north)
	Possessive Adjectives	hotel's (bar)
	Adjective Phrases	(books) in the library
	Adjective Clauses	(the bag)(that) he brought into the aircraft
	Infinitives	(migratory birds) to come to the lake
	Present Particles	(guests) staying at the hotel
	Past Particles	(a clock) mounted on the wall
Adjectives		nocturnal, last (Monday)
of Time	Prepositive Nouns	day (pack)
	Possessive Adjectives	today's (news)
	Adjective Phrases	(a call) at midnight
	Adjective Clauses	(the meeting) (which) we held today
	Infinitives	(days) to come
	Present Particles	passing (time)
	Past Particles	(the summer) gone by
Pro-	Referential	the, a, this, such [quality], my [possession]
Adjectives	Interrogative-Exclamatory	what (color), whose, which
	Relative	whose

Spanish adjectives may be befor or after nouns as we have seen in (13). Nonselective adjectives such as "<u>dulce</u> miel (sweet honey)" are before nouns and selective adjectives such as "salsa <u>dulce</u> (sweat sauce)" are after nouns.

The concordance with the modified nouns facilitates the mobility of word order making explicit their relation.

(28) Spanish Adjectives		Examples
Qualifier		blanco/a, largo/a, grande
Adjectives	Postpositive Nouns	(coche) cama
	Adjective Phrases	(una pintura) de gran valor
	Adjective Clauses	(la puerta) (que) abriste
	Present Particles	(niños) riendo
	Past Particles	(camisa) planchada
Quantifier		mucho/a(s), poco/a(s)
Adjectives	Cardinal Number djectives	un/a, dos, tres
	Multiple Adjectives	doble, triple
Adjectives		urbano, ártico
of Place	Ordinal Number Adjectives	primer(o)/a, segundo/a, tercer(o)/a
	Prepositive Nouns	(viento) norte
	Adjective Phrases	(libros) en la biblioteca
	Adjective Clauses	(el bolso) que él trajo en la aeronave
	Past Particles	(el reloj) montado en la pared
Adjectives		nocturno/a, (el lunes) pasado
of Time	Adjective Phrases	(una llamada) a la medianoche
	Adjective Clauses	(la reunión) que celebramos hoy
	Past Particles	(el verano) pasado
Pro-	Referential	el/la este/a, así [quality], mi
Adjectives		[possession]
	Interrogative-Exclamatory	qué (color), de quién, cuál
	Adjective Clauses	(la reunión) que celebramos hoy
	Past Particles	(el verano) pasado

Chinsese attribute adjectives are characterized with their meanings; 大 dà (big) 小 xiǎo (small) 长 cháng (long) 短 duǎn (short), but any noun may be an adjective before a noun, the same as in English.

(29) Chinese Adjectives		Examples
Qualifier Adjectives		白 bái (white), 长 zhǎng (long), 大 dà (big)
	Prepositive Nouns	邮政 yóuzhèng (post) (局 jú (office))
	Adjective Phrases	(一个 Yīgè(a))伟大 wěidà (great)的 de(of) 价值 jiàzhí(value) 的 de (of) (图片 túpiàn(picture))
	Adjective Clauses	你 nǐ (you)打开 dǎkāi(open)的 de (of) (门 mén(door))
Quantifier Adjectives		很多 hènduō(much), 很少 hěn shǎo (few), 没 méi (no) (钱 qián (money))
	Cardinal Number djectives	一 yī, 二 èr, 三 sān
Adjectives of Place	Ordinal Number Adjectives	第一 dì yī,第二 dì èr,第三 dì sān
	Prepositive Nouns	北 běi(north)风 fēng(wind)
	Adjective Phrases	图书馆 túshū guǎn(library)的 de(of) (书 shū(book))
	Adjective Clauses	他 tā (he)带 dài (have) 来 lái (come) 了 le [perfect particle] 飞机 fēijī (aircraft) 的 de (of) (袋子 dàizi(bag))
Adjectives of Time	Prepositive Nouns	夜间 Yèjiān (nocturnal), 最后 zuìhòu(last) 星期一 xīngqí yī (Monday)), 日 rì(包 bāo(pack))
	Adjective Phrases	在 zài (at) 午夜 wùyè (midnight) 的 de (of) (电话 diànhuà(call))
	Adjective Clauses	我们 wǒmen (we)今天 jīntiān (today) 举行 jǔxíng (held) 的 de (of) (会议 huìyì (meeting))
Pro- Adjectives	Referential	这 zhè(this), 这样的 zhèyàng de (such), 我的 wǒ (I) de(of)
	Interrogative-Exclamatory	什么(shénme) (what) (颜色 yánsè (color)), 谁的 shuí (who) de (of) 哪 nǎ (which)

The proper Japanese adjectives, which end with "いi ", are limited to the basic ones. The derived adjectives from Chinese nouns or European adjectives with "な na" have increased the vocabulary of adjectives; 安全な aNzeNna (safe) (<safety (Chinese) +na,) 、ハードな hādona (hard) etc.

(30) Japanese Adjectives		Examples
Qualifier		白い shiroi (white), 長い nagai (long), 大きい ookii(big)
Adjectives	Prepositive Nouns	郵便 yuubiN (post)局 kyoku (office)
	Adjective Phrases	高値の takane-no (great value-of) 絵 e (picture)
	Adjective Clauses	あなたが開けた anata-ga aketa (you opened) (扉 tobira (door)), 笑っている waratteiru laughing) (子供 kodomo (children))
Quantifier		多い ooi(much/many), 少ない sukunai (a few)
Adjectives	Cardinal Number djectives	一 ichi (one), 二 ni (two), 三 san (three)
Adjectives	Ordinal Number Adjectives	第一 daiichi (no) (first (of)), 第二 daini (no) (second (of)),
of Place		第三 daisaN (no) (third(of))
	Prepositive Nouns	北 kita (north) (風 kaze(wind))
	Adjective Phrases	都市の toshi-no (urban), 北極の hokkyoku-no (arctic)
	Adjective Clauses	彼が飛行機に持ち込んだ(バッグ) kare-ga hikouki-ni mochikoNda (he aircraft-to brought) (baggu(bag))
Adjectives	Adjective Phrases	夜の yoru-no (of night),
of Time		前の mae-no (last) (月曜日 getsuyoubi (Monday)),
	Adjective Clauses	今日あった kyou atta (today was) (会議 kaigi (meeting))
Pro-	Referential Pro-Adjectives	ある aru (a), この kono (this), そんな soNna (such)
Adjectives	Interrogative-Exclamatory	何の nani-no/どんな doNna (what) (色 iro (color)), 誰の dare-no (whose), どの dono (which)

The number of formal Ainu adjectives is very limited, and, most adjectives are adjective clauses in Ainu. For example, the The English adjective "white" is expressed by an adjective clause with the intransitive verb; "be white" and, English "my" is expressed with "which I have" in Ainu.

(31) Ainu Adjectives		Examples
Qualifier	Prepositive Nouns	soya (cise) (bee (house); beehive)
Adjectives	Adjective Clauses	retar (be white), tanne (be long), poro (be big), e=maka (apa) (you opened (door))
Quantifier	Adjective Clauses	poro (be much/many), pon (be a little)
Adjectives	Cardinal Number djectives	sine (one), tu (two), re(three)
Adjectives	Prepositive Nouns	matnaw(noth (wind)) (rera (wind))
of Place	Ordinal Number djectives	iyotta(first)
	Adjective Clauses	kotan-kor-(cicap)(village-posess-(bird)); owl, a=e-ramu-sarak- (one=by-heart-?) (pe (thing)); anxiety,
Adjectives	Prepositive Nouns	kunne (night) (cup (sun/moon)); moon
of Time	Adjective Clauses	tap-an (now and here-be)
Pro-	Referential	nea (the), tapan(this), toan(that), panko (such), ku= (my)
Adjectives	Interrogative-Exclamatory	hemanta (kamiasi) (what (ghost)), hemanta kor ((that) who has; whose), inan(which)

c. Adverbs

The adverb derives from the adjective in most languages, in German they take even the same form, as the former analyses a thing in quality, quantity, place and time and the later analyses the change of a thing, which may be attributed also quality, quantity, place and time.

The adverbs of time are frequently without prepositions or postpositions, as the vocabulary of one-dimensional time is limited and explicit, different from the rich vocabulary or place, which makes use of anything in three-dimensional simultaneous variation.

(32) English Adverbs		Examples
Qualifier		slowly, perfectly
Adverbs	Nouns without Prepositions	(I did it) the way you told me.
	Adverb Phrases	by bus, with pleasure
	Adverb Clauses	if it rains, as he was young
	Present Particles	(walk) singing
	Past Particles	given the oportunity, (he ...)
Quantifier		much, little, not
Adverbs	Multiple Adverb Phrase	once, twice
Adverbs		up, down, out
of Place	Nouns without Prepositions	(go) home, (come) this way
	Adverb Phrases	on the ground, (bear) in mind
	Adverb Clauses	where he lives
	Infinitives [with *to*]	(come) to see
	Infinitives [without *to*]	(they are going to) marry
	Present Particles	being here in London
	Past Particles	stuck in the airport
Adverbs		now, always
of Time	Nouns without Prepositions	today, tomorrow, (wait) (for) a minute
	Adverb Phrases	in the afternoon, in May
	Adverb Clauses	when the morning sun rises
	Infinitives [with *to*]	till to be found
	Infinitives [without *to*]	to be twenty years old
	Present Particles	starting new semester
	Past Particles	ended September
Pro-	Referential	here [place], then [time], thus [quality]
Adverbs	Interrogative-Exclamatory	where, when, how, why
	Relative	where, when, how, why

Spanish adverbs are more analytic and applicable to allow the form such as "rápida y correctamente" (rapidly and correctly) than English adverbs, as they derive with a female Latin noun "mens" (mind) in concordance.

(33) Spanish Adverbs		Examples
Qualifier Adverbs		despacio, perfectamente
	Adjective Phrases	en autobús, con placer
	Adjective Clauses	si llueve, como él era joven
	Present Particles	(anda) cantando
	Past Particles	dada la oportunidad, (él ...)
Quantifier Adverbs		mucho, poco, no
	Multiple Adverb Phrase	una vez, dos veces
Adverbs of Place		arriba, abajo, fuera
	Adjective Phrases	en la tierra, (tener) en cuenta
	Adjective Clauses	donde él vive
	Present Particles	estando aquí en Londres
	Past Particles	atrapado en el aeropuerto
Adverbs of Time		ahora, siempre
	Nouns without Prepositions	hoy, mañana, (espera) un momento
	Adjective Phrases	por la tarde, en Mayo
	Adjective Clauses	cuando sale el sol
	Present Particles	comenzando el nuevo semestre
Pro-Adverbs	Referential	aquí [place], entonces [time], así [quality]
	Interrogative-Exclamatory	dónde, cuándo, cómo, por qué
	Relative	donde, cuando, como, por (lo) que/cual

Chinese adverbs do not always correspond to English adverbs, sometimes they are direct objects. For example, "I go to Shanghai" is "我 wǒ (I) 去 qù (go) 上海 Shànghǎi (SVO), the same as "I leave Shanghai. (SVO)", though "I live in Shanghai" is "我 wǒ (I) 住 zhù (live) 在上海 zài Shànghǎi (in Shanghai). (SV+Av-P)".

(34) Chinese Adverbs		Examples
Qualifier Adverbs	Adverb Phrases	坐巴士 zuò bāshì (by bus)
	Adverb Clauses	如果 Rúguǒ (if) 下雨 xià yǔ (rains),
		因为 yīnwèi (as) 他 tā (he) 很 hěn (very) 年轻 niánqīng (young)
Quantifier Adverbs		很多 hěnduō (much), 不大 bù dà (not much=little) 不 bù /没 méi (not)
	Multiple Adverb Phrase	一次 yīcì (once), 两次 liǎng cì (twice)
Adverbs of Place		上 shàng (up), 下 xià (down), 出 chū (out)
	Adverb Phrases	在 zài (on) 地上 dìshàng (ground),
		他 tā (he) 住 zhù (live) 的 dì (of) 地方 dìfāng (place)
Adverbs of Time		现在 xiànzài(now), 总是 zǒng shì (then)
	Nouns without Prepositions	今天 jīntiān (today), 明天 míngtiān (tomorrow),
		(等 děng (wait))一 yī (one) 分 fēn (minute) 钟 zhōng (for)
	Adverb Phrases	在 zài (in) 五 wǔ (five)月 yuè (moon), 当 dāng (moment) 太阳 tàiyáng (sun)
Pro-Adverbs	Referential	这 zhè (this)里 lǐ (place), 当 dāng (that) 时 shí (time), 从而 cóng'ér (thus)
	Interrogative-Exclamatory	在哪里 zài nǎlǐ (whwew),何时 hé shí (when),
		如何 rúhé (how), 为什么 wèishéme (why)

Almost all the Japanese verbs and adjectives derive to adverbs named RENTAIKEI. In addition, we find many onomatopoeic adverbs, as things make sounds when they move.

(35) Japanese Adverbs		Examples
Qualifier Adverbs		ゆっくり(と) yukkuri (-to) (slowly), 完全に kaNzeNni (perfectly)
	Adverb Phrases	バスで basu de (bus by)
	Adverb Clauses	もし雨が降ったら moshi ame-ga huttara (if rain fall),
		彼は若かったので kore-wa wakakatta-node (he young-was as)
Quantifier Adverbs		たくさん takusaN(much), 少し sukoshi (a little)
	Multiple Adverb Phrase	一回 ikkai(once), 二回 nikai(twice)
Adverbs of Place	Adverb Phrases	上に ue-ni (up), 下に sita-ni (down), 外に soto-ni (out)
Adverbs of Time		いつも istumo (always)
	Nouns without Prepositions	今 ima (now), 今日 kyou (today), 明日 ashita (tomorrow)
	Adverb Phrases	午後に gogo-ni (afternoon-in), 五月に gogatsu-ni (May-in)
	Adverb Clauses	朝日が昇るとき asahi-ga noboru toki (morning-sun rise when),
Pro-Adverbs	Referential	ここ koko (here), そのとき sonotoki (then),
		そのように sonoyouni (thus)
	Interrogative-Exclamatory	どこで doko-de (where), いつ itsu (when),
		どのように donoyouni (how), なぜ naze (why)

In Ainu we find many adverbs derived from verbs, which include the intransitive combinations of the verb "be + adjective".

(36) Ainu Adverbs		Examples
Qualifier		ratci (slowly), sino (truly), nesi(perfectly) [particle]
Adverbs	Adverb Phrases	makiri ani (knife with)
	Adverb Clauses	apto as (rain do) hike(if), okkayo (man) pewre (be young) kusu (because), ku=sinotcaki kor (I=sing –ing) (ku=apkas) (I=walk)
Quantifier		earkinne (much), ponno (a little), somo (not)
Adverbs	Adverb Particle	(arpa(go)) ranke (repeatedly)
Adverbs	Adverb Phrases	toy or ta (ground place on), tun ehotke hi ta (two sleep place at)
of Place		(where the two sleep)
Adverbs		tane (now), ranma (always), iruka (for a
of Time		minute)(en=tere(me=wait))
	Nouns without Prepositions	tanto(today), nisatta (tomorrow)
	Adverb Phrases	tokap-ipe oka ta (day-food (;luch) after at; in the afternoon), mo-maw-ta-cup ta (calm wind with moon in; in May)
Pro-	Referential	te ta (here at), teta (recently), enepo (thus)
Adverbs	Interrogative-Exclamatory	hunak ta (where at), hempar (when), mak (how), hemanta kusu (what for; why)

d. Pro-Modifiers

In the traditional formal grammar, both the modifier of the adjective; "perfectly (good)", and, the modifier of the adverb; "perfectly (well)" are regarded as adverbs for the coincidence of the form; "(He did it) perfectly". However, they are different parts of speech.

As Ainu adjectives and adverbs are mainly clauses, we could not find any pro-modifiers in our Ainu text.

(37) English Ad-Modifiers		Examples
Ad-Adj		very (good), somewhat (short)
Pro-Ad-	Referential	so (nice)
Adjectives	Interrogative-Exclamatory	how (deep the river is)
Ad-Adv		very (early), somewhat (late)
Pro-Ad-	Referential	so (easily)
Adverbs	Interrogative-Exclamatory	how (much)

(38) Spanish Ad-Modifiers		Examples
Ad-Adj		muy (bueno), un poco (corto)
Pro-Ad-Adjectives	Referential Pro-Ad-Adjectives	tan (bueno)
	Interrogative-Exclamatory Pro-Ad- Adjectives	cuán (profundo es el río)
Ad-Adv		muy (temprano), un poco (tarde)
Pro-Ad-Adverbs	Referential Pro-Ad-Adverbs	tan (fácilmente)

(39) Chinese Ad-Modifiers		Examples
Ad-Adj		很 hěn (very) (好 hǎo (good)), 有点 yǒudiǎn (somewhat) (短 duǎn (short))
Pro-Ad-Adjectives	Referential	所以 suǒyǐ (so) 很 hěn (very) (好 hǎo (good))
Ad-Adv		很 hěn (very) (早 zǎo(early),) 有点 yǒudiǎn (somewhat) (迟 chí (late)
Pro-Ad-Adverbs	Referential	所以 suǒyǐ (so) 很 hěn (very) (容易(róngyì))

(40) Japanese Ad-Modifiers		Examples
Ad-Adj		とても totemo (very) (よい yoi (good)), いくらか ikuraka (somewhat) (短い mijikai (short))
Pro-Ad-Adjectives	Referential	そんなに soNnani (so) (素敵な sutekina (nice))
	Interrogative /Exclamatory	[interr.] どれくらい dorekurai (how) (深い川か hukai kawa ka (deep river [interrogative particle]) [exclam.] なんと naNto (how) (深い川だ hukai kawa da (deep river is))
Ad-Adv		とても totemo (very)(早く (early)), いくらか ikuraka (somewhat) (遅く(late))
Pro-Ad-Adverbs	Referential	そんなに soNnani (so) (簡単に kaNtaNni (easily))
	Interrogative-Exclamatory	どれくらい dorekurai (how) (多く ooku (much))

4) Full Sentence Examples

We will look at an example of full sentence composed of SVOI in each language, which is not found easily in real utterances.

(41) English
I told him something that he didn't want to hear.

(Winston Groom. *Forest Gamp*.)

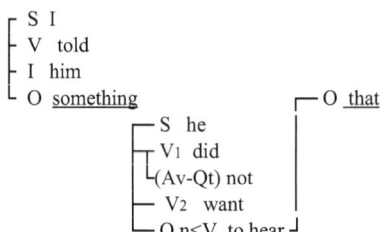

```
┌ S  I
├ V  told
├ I  him
└ O  something          ┌─ O  that
              ┌─ S  he
            ┌─┤ V₁  did
            │ └(Av-Qt) not
            ├─ V₂  want
            └─ O n<V  to hear ┘
```

(42) Spanish
César Montero se dejó requisar, impasible, con los brazos abiertos.
César Montero let himself be examined, impassive, with arms open.

(Gabriel García Márquez. *La mala hora*.)

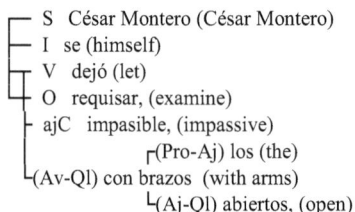

```
┌─ S  César Montero (César Montero)
├─ I  se (himself)
┌─┤ V  dejó (let)
└─┤ O  requisar, (examine)
  ├ ajC  impasible, (impassive)
  │           ┌(Pro-Aj) los (the)
  └(Av-Ql) con brazos  (with arms)
             └(Aj-Ql) abiertos, (open)
```

(43) Chinese
过生日时，他买了一个最新的MP4给我.   (NHK Radio Text (2008) *Every Day Chinese*.)
Guò shēngri shí,tā mǎile yíge zuì xīn de MP sì gěi wǒ.
On birthday, he bought a new mp4 and gave it to me.

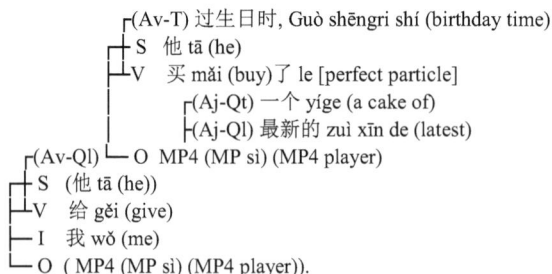

```
          ┌(Av-T) 过生日时, Guò shēngri shí (birthday time)
         ┌┤ S  他 tā (he)
         └┤V  买 mǎi (buy) 了 le [perfect particle]
          │      ┌(Aj-Qt) 一个 yíge (a cake of)
          │      ├(Aj-Ql) 最新的 zuì xīn de (latest)
  ┌(Av-Ql) └─ O  MP4 (MP sì) (MP4 player)
 ┌┤ S  (他 tā (he))
 └┤V  给 gěi (give)
  ├ I  我 wǒ (me)
  └ O  ( MP4 (MP sì) (MP4 player)).
```

(44) Japanese

ジープに乗った少尉は、遠まきに見ている人びとに、手を振った。

jiipu-ni notta shoui-wa, toomaki-ni miteiru hitobito-ni, te-o hutta.The second lieutenant in a jeep waved a hand to people who were looking at a distance in a wide circle around him. (SAKI Ryuuzou, "Hi-no naka-ni kieta" (Disappeared in the fire))

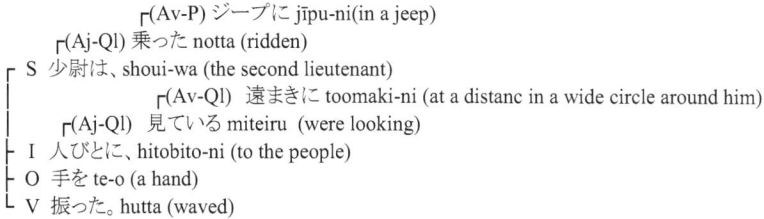

```
                    ┌(Av-P) ジープに jīpu-ni(in a jeep)
              ┌(Aj-Ql) 乗った notta (ridden)
    ┌  S 少尉は、shoui-wa (the second lieutenant)
    │                   ┌(Av-Ql) 遠まきに toomaki-ni (at a distanc in a wide circle around him)
    │        ┌(Aj-Ql) 見ている miteiru  (were looking)
    ├  I 人びとに、hitobito-ni (to the people)
    ├  O 手を te-o (a hand)
    └  V 振った。hutta (waved)
```

(45) Ainu

tu pirka itak re pirka itak ye kor earkinne a=kor nispa kasi a=osike ayne ora

Saying good words many times I made my husband a gift sincerely and,

("Famine and a crow god" *Folktales by UEDA Toshi 3*)

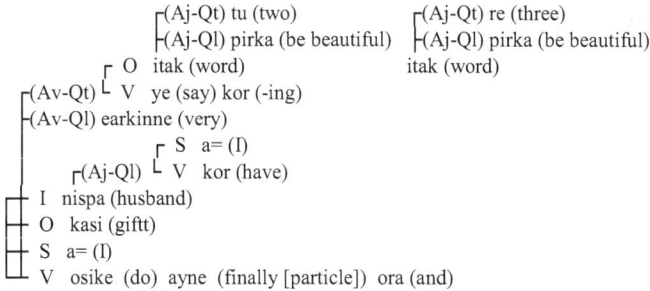

```
              ┌(Aj-Qt) tu (two)          ┌(Aj-Qt) re (three)
              ├(Aj-Ql) pirka (be beautiful)  ├(Aj-Ql) pirka (be beautiful)
         ┌  O  itak (word)              itak (word)
   ┌(Av-Qt) └  V  ye (say) kor (-ing)
   ├(Av-Ql) earkinne (very)
   │                    ┌ S  a= (I)
   │        ┌(Aj-Ql) └ V  kor (have)
   ├  I  nispa (husband)
   ├  O  kasi (giftt)
   ├  S  a= (I)
   └  V  osike (do) ayne (finally [particle]) ora (and)
```

2 Mobility

The English and Chinese basic word orders; (7) (9), may change when the direct and indirect objects are with prepositions.

The Spanish components can move freely, as the subject is marked in the conjugation, the animate direct object, the candidate of the subject, is distinguished with the preposition "a" and the indirect object is always with a preposition (8).

The Japanese noun components, all of which are with particles, may move freely, but, the verb finishes the sentence always in the end (10).

On the other hand, the word order of Ainu component is fixed because of the absence of markers (11).

(46) English
- S John
- V-s sends
- O flowers
- x-I to Mary.

(47) Chinese1
- S 张伟 Zhāng Wěi
- x-O 把 bǎ 花 huā (flowers)
- V 送 sòng 了 le (have send)
- I 王芳. Wáng Fang

(48) Chinese2
- S 张伟 Zhāng wěi
- x-I 给 gěi 王芳 Wáng Fang
- V 送 sòng
- O 花 . huā.

3 Pronominalization

English and Chinese pronouns serve to keep grammatical word order. Spanish pronouns redundantly make explicit the grammatical function of words, which may move freely.

In Japanese substitution of words is regarded as impolite or rude. We think that we should not call a man or thing in pronoun, but in its proper name if it has a name. As even "あなた anata (you)" may sound belligerent depending on context, we generally use the proper name of the 2nd person; 田中さん Tanaka-san (Mr./Ms. Tanaka). The same mentality can be also seen also in things as well.

Though verbs take clitic pronouns in Ainu, pronouns of the 3rd person are not used generally. Different form Japanese they use more common generic nouns like "okkayo (man)" than his proper name.

(49) English 1
- S He
- V-s sends
- I her
- O flowers.

(50) English 2
- S He
- V-s sends
- O them
- x-I to her.

(51) English 3 (England)
- S He
- V-s sends
- O them
- I her.

(52) Spanish 1
- S El
- O las
- V-s envía
- x-I a María.

(53) Spanish 2
- S El
- I le
- V-s envía
- O flowers.

(54) Spanish 3
- S El
- I le
- V-s envía
- O flowers
- x-I a María.

(55) Spanish 4
```
┌ S   El
├ I   se
├ O   las
└ V-s  envía.
```

(56) Spanish 5
```
┌ S   El
├ I   se
├ O   las
├ V  -s envía.
└ x-I  a María.
```

(57) Chinese 1
```
┌ S  他 Tā
├ V  送
├ I  她 tā
└ O  那个. nàge
```

(58) Chinese 2
```
┌ S  他 Tā
├ x-O  把 bǎ 那个 nàge
├ V  送 sòng 了 le (have send)
└ I  她. tā
```

(59) Chinese 3
```
┌ S  他 Tā
├ x-I  给 gěi 她 tā
├ V  送 sòng
└ O  那个. nàge
```

(60) Chinese 4
```
┌ S  他 Tā
├ x-O  把 bǎ 那个 nàge
├ V  送 sòng 了 le
└ x-I  给 gěi 她 tā.
```

(61) Japanese
```
┌ S-x  彼が kare-ga
├ I-x  彼女に kanojo-ni
├ O-x  それを sore-o
└ V   送る。okuru
```

(62) Ainu 1
```
┌ I+3  Sátamo
├ O+3  nonno
├ S-3  ku= (I)
└ V   eikra
```

(63) Ainu2
```
┌ O+3  nonno
├ I-3  e= (you)
├ S-3  ku= (I)
└ V   eikra.(send)
```

(64) Ainu 3
```
┌ I+3  Sátamo (to Sátamo)
├ O-3  e= (you)
├ S-3  ku= (I)
└ V   uamkirre. (present)
```

4 Interrogation

1) Total Interrogation

The characteristic of English interrogation is the inversion of word order of subjects and verbs. To keep this order the dummy auxiliary verbs are put at the top.

Spanish interrogative sentences begin with the reversed question mark, as they do not have formal characteristic of the freedom of word order.

Chinese, Japanese and Ainu interrogative sentences are characterized with the interrogative particle in the end.

(65) English
```
┌ Ax  Dose
├ S   John
├ V-s  send
├ I   Mary
└ O   flowers?
```

(66) Spanish
```
┌ S   ¿ Juan
├ V-s  envía
├ O   flores
└ x-I  a María?
```

23

(67) Chinese 1
```
┌ S   张伟 Zhāng Wěi
├ V   送 sòng
├ I   王芳 Wáng Fang
└ O   花 吗? huā ma
```

(68) Chinese 2
```
┌ S   张伟 Zhāng Wěi
├ V   送 sòng
│ ┌(Av-Qt) 不 bu
├┴ V   送 sòng
├ I   王芳 Wáng Fang
└ O   花 吗? huā ma
```

(69) Japanese
```
┌ S-x  弘が Hiroshi-ga
├ I-x  洋子に Yoko-ni
├ O-x  花を hana-o
└ V   送るか。okuru-ka
```

(70) Ainu
```
┌ S+3  Nanke'aynu
├ I+3  Sátamo
├ O+3  nonno
└ V   eikra ya?
```

2) Partial Interrogation

The partial interrogative substitutes should be at the top in English and Spanish, but not in Chinese, Japanese and Ainu.

(71) English
```
┌ O+Q  What
├ Ax-s dose
├ S   John
├ V   send
└ I   to Mary?
```

(72) Spanish
```
┌ O+Q  ¿ Qué
├ V   envía
├ S   Juan
└ x-I  a María?
```

(73) Chinese
```
┌ S   张伟 Zhāng Wěi
├ V   送 sòng
├ I   王芳 Wáng Fang
└ O+Q  什么? shénme
```

(74) Japanese
```
┌ S-x   弘が Hiroshi-ga
├ I-x   洋子に Yoko-ni
├ O+Q -x 何を nani-o
└ V    送る。okuru
```

(75) Ainu
```
┌ S+3   Nanke'aynu
├ I+3   Sátamo
├ O+Q   hemanta
└ V    eikra?
```

5 Negation

In the five languages the negation of the sentence is the negation of the verb, whiche relates all the components expressing the change.

(76) English
```
 ┌─ S   John
 ├─ Ax-s  does
 │┌(Av-Qt) not
 └┴ V-s   send
 ├─ I   Mary
 └─ O   flowers.
```

(77) Spanish
```
 ┌─ S   Juan
 │┌(Av-Qt) no
 └┴ V-s   envía
 ├─ O   flores
 └─ x-I  a María.
```

(78) Chinese
```
 ┌─ S   张伟 Zhāng Wěi
 │┌(Av-Qt) 不 bu
 └┴ V   送 sòng
 ├─ I   王芳 Wáng Fang
 └─ O   花. huā
```

(79) Japanese
```
 ┌ S-x  弘が Hiroshi-ga
 ├ I-x  洋子に Yoko-ni
 ├ O-x  花を hana-o
 └ V-Ax 送らない。okura-nai
```

(80) Ainu
```
                ┌ S+3  Nanke'aynu
                ├ I+3  Sátamo
                ├ O+3  nonno
      ┌─ O+3   └ V  eikra
     ┌│┌(Av-Qt) somo (not)
     └└┴ V  ki. (do)
```

6 Intransitives S=O

When the subject is not identical with the indirect object, the verb is transitive to change the other. When the subject is identical with the indirect object, the verb is intransitive to change oneself.

For the identity with the subject, the reflexive direct objects of intransitive verbs are not expressed in many languages, if the end of the change is not emphasized. On the other hand, the direct objects of transitive verbs are expressed generally, because they are not identical with the subjects. The distinction between the transitive and intransitive is not in the appearance of direct object, but in the identity of subject and direct object.

Chinese adjectives and adverbs in main affirmative sentences are almost always with *hěn* (very) to finish the sentence.

(81) English
```
 ┌─ S   I
 │┌ V-s  get
 └┼ O   (me)
 ├(Av-P) up
 └(Av-T) early.
```

(82) Spanish
```
 ┌─ S   (yo)
 ├─ O   Me
 └─ V-s  levanto
 └(Av-T) temprano.
```

(83) Chinese
```
 ┌─ S   我 Wǒ
 │┌(Av-Qt) 很 hěn (very)早就 zǎo jiù (early)
 └┴ V   起床 qǐchuáng.
        (get up from bed)
```

(84) Japanese
```
┌─ S-x 私が watashi-ga
├┌(Av-Qt) 早く hayaku
└└ V 起きる。okiru
```
  * transitive 他動詞 : 起こす okosu

(85) Ainu
```
 ┌(Av-T) nokunneywano (early morning)
 ├ S-3  ku= (I)
 ├ O+3  ho- ((my) hip)
 └ V   puni. (raise)
```

7 *A is B* (Noun)

The following examples have the sentence pattern SVC or SCV to express the static attributes of the subject in a noun, which is a bundle of adjectives.

(86) English
```
┌─ S  John
└┬ V-s  is
 └ nC  a sailor.
```

(87) Spanish
```
┌─ S  Juan
└┬ V-s  es
 └ nC  marinero.
```

(90) Ainu
```
┌─ S    Nanke'ainu
├┌ nC   cip-o-kur (boat-board-man)
└└ V    ne.
```

8 *A is B* (Adjective)

The verb "be" is absent in present tense with adjective complement in Chinese and Japanese. Chinese adjective complements take 很 (hen) to show that the word is not a noun but an adjective. The verb appears in the colloquial polite form with "です (desu)" and in past tense.

All the Ainu qualifier adjectives are adjective clause composed of the verb "be" and adjective. Therefore, the sentence pattern SVajC/SajCV in other languages is SV in Ainu.

(91) English
```
┌─ S  John
└┬ V-s  is
 └ ajC  smart.
```

(92) Spanish1
```
┌─ S  Juan
└┬ V-s  es
 └ ajC  inteligente.
```

(93) Spanish1
```
┌─ S  Juan
└┬ V-s  está [+temporary]
 └ ajC  enfermo. (sick)
```

(94) Chinese
```
┌─ S   张伟 Zhāng Wěi
└┬ V   Ø
 └ ajC  很聪明. hěn (very) cōngmíng
```

(95) Japanese1
- S-x 弘は Hiroshi-wa(determiner)
  - ajC 賢い kashikoi
- V （です desu [polite])。

(96) Japanese 2
- S-x 弘は Hiroshi-wa(determiner)
  - ajC 賢 kashiko-
- V かった。 katta (<-ku-at(be)-tta(past))

(97) Ainu
- S   Nanke'ainu
- V   ramu-an. (heart-be (be wise))

9 *A is B* (Adverb)

In Ainu only *ne* (the) distinguishes "There is a house on the hill" and "The house is on the hill".

(98) English
- S   The house
- V-s is
- avC   on the hill.

(99) Spanish
- S   La casa
- V-s está
- avC en la colina.

(100) Chinese
- S   房子 fángzi
- V   Ø
- avC 在山上. zài shān shàng (on hill top)

(101) Japanese1
- S   その家は sono (that) ie (house)-wa (determiner)
  - avC 丘の上に oka-no ue-ni (hill-of top-at)
- V   ある。 aru (be [-animate])

(102) Japanese 2
- S   その人は sono (that) hito (man)-wa (determiner)
  - nC 丘の上に oka-no ue-ni (hill-of top-at)
- V   いる。 iru (be [+animate])

(103) Ainu
- (Av-P) toska ka ta (hill top at)
- S   ne cise (the house)
- V   an. (be)

10 *There be*

In English we see verb-second (V2) word order common to other German languages. In the following example the first "there" is a dummy to make a V2 structure; "There is not much cover there to conceal anything "(Greene, Graham, *The Heart of the Matter.*)

The subject of Spanish and Chinese "someone" never appears in the surface structure.

(104) English
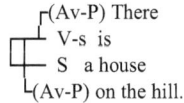
   (Av-P) There
   V-s is
   S   a house
   (Av-P) on the hill.

(105) Spanish
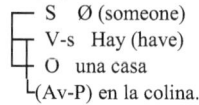
   S   Ø (someone)
   V-s Hay (have)
   O   una casa
   (Av-P) en la colina.

(106) Chinese
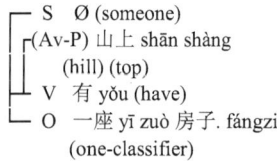
   S   Ø (someone)
   (Av-P) 山上 shān shàng
     (hill) (top)
   V 有 yǒu (have)
   O 一座 yī zuò 房子. fángzi
     (one-classifier)

(107) Japanese1
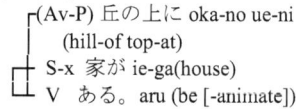
   (Av-P) 丘の上に oka-no ue-ni
     (hill-of top-at)
   S-x 家が ie-ga(house)
   V ある。 aru (be [-animate])

(108) Japanese 2
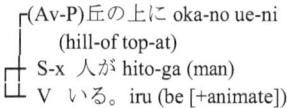
   (Av-P)丘の上に oka-no ue-ni
     (hill-of top-at)
   S-x 人が hito-ga (man)
   V いる。 iru (be [+animate])

(109) Ainu
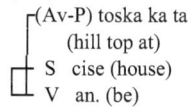
   (Av-P) toska ka ta
     (hill top at)
   S cise (house)
   V an. (be)

11 Imperatives

The presupposed subject in 2nd person in imperative sentences does not appear in most cases. However, the subjects may appear much more in Spanish, in which the 2nd person may be singular or plural, each have a polite 3rd person form "usted (es)".

(110) English
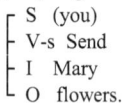
   S   (you)
   V-s Send
   I   Mary
   O   flowers.

(111) Spanish1
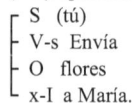
   S   (tú)
   V-s Envía
   O   flores
   x-I a María.

(112) Spanish2
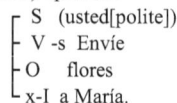
   S   (usted[polite])
   V -s Envíe
   O   flores
   x-I a María.

(113) Chinese
```
┌ S  (你 nǐ)
├ V  送 sòng
├ I  王芳 Wáng Fāng
└ O  花. huā
```

(114) Japanese
```
┌ S-x  (あなたが anata-ga )
├ I-x  洋子に Yoko-ni
├ O-x  花を hana-o
└ V-Ax  送れ oku-re
      /送りなさい。okuri-nasai [polite]
```

(115) Ainu
```
┌ I+3  Sátamo
├ O+3  nonno
├ ProS-3  (e=)
└ V   eikra (yan [polite]).
```

12 Negative Imperatives

In Japanese and Ainu the negative imperative is not the combination and negation and imperatives, but it is expressed with proper elements "な (na)" and "iteke" respectively.

(116) English
```
┌ S  (you)
├ Ax-s  Do
├┌(Av-Qt) not
│└ V-s  send
├ I  Mary
└ O  flowers.
```

(117) Spanish
```
┌ S  (tú)
├┌(Av-Qt) No
│└ V-s  envies
├ O  flores
└ x-I  a María.
```

(118) Chinese
```
┌ S  (你 nǐ)
│┌(Av-Qt) 不 bu
│└ V  送 sòng
├ I  王芳 Wáng Fāng
└ O  花. huā
```

(119) Japanese
```
┌ S-x  (あなたが anata-ga )
├ I-x  洋子に Yoko-ni
├ O-x  花を hana-o
└ V-Ax  送るな。okuru-na
```

(120) Ainu
```
┌ I+3  Sátamo
├ O+3  nonno
│┌(Av-Qt) iteke(not) [imperative]
│└ V  eikra. (send)
```

13 Indefinite Subjects

The Spanish 3rd personal pronoun "se" is the most adequate to the indefinite subject, as it is used as both male and female and both singular and plural direct and indirect objects.

Ainu indefinite subject "an" means "I" in indirect narration, which is the style of Ainu folktales.

(121) English
```
┌ S  Everyone
├ V-s  wants
└ O   to live
      └(Av-Ql) in peace.
```

(122) Spanish
```
┌ ProS  Se
├ V-s  quiere
└ O  vivir
      └(Av-Ql) en paz.
```

(123) Chinese
```
 ┌ S  每个人都 měi gèrén dōu
 ├ V  希望 xīwàng
 └ O  生活 shēnghuó
     └(Aj-Ql) 在和平. zài hépíng
```

(124) Japanese
```
 ┌ ProS-x 誰もが dare-mo-ga(who even)
 │ ┌(Av-Ql) 平和に heiwa-ni
 └└V-Ax 暮らしたい。 kurashi-tai(want)
```

(125) Ainu
```
 ┌(Av-Ql) apunno (quietly)
 ┌┴ plV  oka (live)
 └ ProS-3  =an (every one) rusuy. (want [particle]))
```

14 Passive

Passive is a state generally expressed with the verb "be" and past particle as a result of the change. In the example Spanish2 we see another form of personification to hide the agent. As Chinese words do not conjugate nor inflect, the passive is not characterized by the structure, but the agent and the perfect tense.

In Chinese and Japanese the passive is not frequent because it tends to mean bad results.

(126) English1
```
 ┌ S   Flowers
 ┬ V   are
 ├ ajC  sent
 ┴(av-Ql) by John
 └ x-I  to Mary.
```

(127) English2
```
 ┌ S   Mary
 ┬ V   is
 └ ajC  sent flowers
        └(av-Ql) by John .
```

(128) Spanish1
```
 ┌ S   Flores
 ┬ V   son
 ├ ajC  enviadas
 ┴ x-I  a María.
 └(av-Ql) por Juan.
```

(129) Spanish2
```
 ┌ O   Se [reflexive]
 ├ V   envían
 └ S   flores.
```

(130) Chinese
```
 ┌ S  花 huā
 │ ┌(Av-Ql) 被 bèi 张伟 Zhāng Wěi
 ├┴ V 送 了 le (have send)
 └ I  王芳. Wáng Fāng
```

(131) Japanese 1
```
 ┌ S-x 花が haga-ga
 │ ┌(Av-P) 弘から Hiroshi-kara
 ├┤ I-x 洋子に Yoko-ni
 └└ V-Ax 送られる。 okurareru
```

(132) Japanese2
```
┌─ S-x  洋子が Yoko-gai
│ ┌(Av-Ql) 弘に Hiroshi-ni (yotte; by)
├─┤ O-x  花を hana-o
└┴─ V-Ax 送られる。okurareru
```

(133) Japanese3
```
┌─ S-x  弘が Hiroshi-ga
│ ┌(Av-Ql) 赤ん坊に akaNbou-ni (by baby)
└┴─ V-Ax 泣かれる。nakareru (be cried)
```

(134) Ainu
```
 ┌(Av-P) Nanke'aynu or (place) wa(from)
┌┤ I+3   Sátamo
├┤ O+3   nonno
├┤ ProS-3 en= (one<we all)
└┴─ V    eikra. (send)
```

15 Causative, Permission and Petition

The causative, permission and petition take the same sentence structure in English, Spanish and Chinese. However, in Japanese and Ainu there is not formal distinction between the causative and the permission, and the sentence structure of the petition is another.

(135) English
```
┌ S   John
├ V-s makes
│     /lets/asks
├ I   Mary
└ O   go.
```

(136) Spanish
```
┌ S   Juan
├ V-s hace
│     /deja/pide
├ O   ir
└ x-I a María.
```

(137) Chinese
```
┌ S 张伟 Zhāng Wěi
├ V 叫 jiào /让 ràng/请 qǐng
├ I (给 gěi) 王芳 Wáng Fang
└ O 去. qù
```

(138) Japanese1
```
┌ S-x    弘が Hiroshi-ga
├ I-x/O-x 洋子に/を Yoko-ni/o
└ V-Ax  行かせる。ikaseru (make/let)
```

(139) Japanese 2
  ┌ S-x 弘が Hiroshi-ga
  ├ I-x 洋子に Yoko-ni
  │ ┌(Av-Ql) 行くように iku (go) youni (in order to)
  └ V 頼む。 tanomu (ask)

(140) Ainu1
  ┌S+3 Nanke'aynu
  ├I+3 Sátamo
  └ V arpare. (make/let)

(141) Ainu 2
  ┌S+3 Nanke'aynu
  ├I+3 Sátamo
  │┌(Av-Ql) arpa (go) kusu (in order to)
  └ V yeykonisuk. (ask in Chitose)

16 Perceptive

The sentence structure of perceptive SVOC is common in English, Spanish and Chinese. On the other hand, the modifier of the verb; C, is expressed in the modifier of the direct object in Japanese and Ainu.

(142)English
  ┌ S John
  ├ V-s sees
  ├ O Mary
  └ n/avC run/runnig.

(143) Spanish
  ┌ S Juan
  ├ V-s ve
  ├ O a María
  └ n/av C correr/corriendo.

(144) Chinese
  ┌ S 张伟 Zhāng Wěi
  ├ V 看 kàn
  └ O   ┌ S 王芳 Wáng Fang
        └ V 跑. pǎo

(145) Japanese
  ┌ S -x 弘が Hiroshi-ga
  │   ┌ S-x 洋子が Yoko-ga
  │   ┌(Aj-Ql) └ V 走る hashiru
  ├ O-x のを no-o (thing)
  └ V 見る。 miru

(146) Ainu
                ┌S+3 Sátamo
        ┌(Aj-Ql) └ V hoyupu (run)
  ┌ O siri (manner)
  ├ S+3 Nanke'aynu
  └ V nukar.(see)